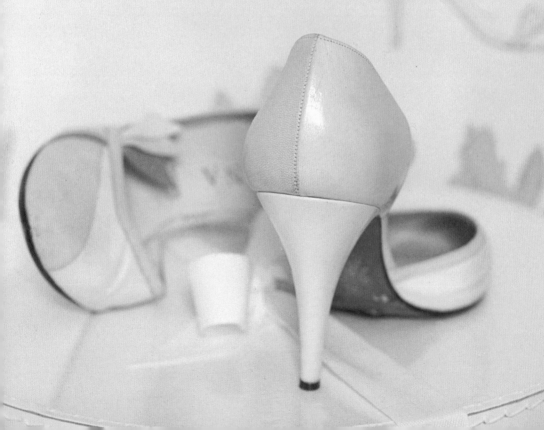

High
heel
heaven

High heel heaven

The glamour and seduction of fabulous shoes

Tracy Martin

LONDON • NEW YORK

Design, Styling and Photographic Art Direction Luis Peral-Aranda

Project Editor Ellen Parnavelas

Copy Editor Zia Mattocks

Production Meskerem Berhane

Art Director Leslie Harrington

Editorial Director Julia Charles

Indexer Hilary Bird

First published in 2013 by
Ryland Peters & Small,
20–21 Jockey's Fields,
London WC1R 4BW

and

519 Broadway, 5th Floor,
New York, NY10012

www.rylandpeters.com

10 9 8 7 6 5 4 3 2 1

ISBN: 978 1 84975 444 6

A CIP record for this book is available from
the British Library.

Library of Congress Cataloging-in-
Publication data has been applied for.

Printed in China.

Contents

Introduction

'Oh my God! Do you know what these are? Manolo Blahnik Mary Janes! I thought these were an urban shoe myth!', shrieked Carrie Bradshaw, the shoe-loving fashionista from *Sex and the City*.

The black patent Campari heel, to which Bradshaw refers in Season 4 of the show, is a minimalist classic that was first created by Blahnik in 1994. The simplistic yet sophisticated styling, with slender stiletto heel, has become iconic, which is why Bradshaw's heart raced as she put them on stating, 'If they don't fit, I am going to wear them anyway.'

Long gone are the days when shoes were viewed simply as a practical necessity for protecting the feet. They are now regarded as entrancing works of art, transporting us into high heel heaven. Shoes call to us, and the minute the perfect pair is spotted there is no going back, as they just have to be bought, worn and loved.

Fortunately, there is a pair to appeal to every shoeaholic's taste, with an abundance of choice, from the slender stiletto to the more robust platform. Some are lavishly embellished for those with extrovert personalities; others are timeless classics that suit the more demure.

As Marilyn Monroe famously quoted, 'Give a girl the right shoe and she can conquer the world.' No truer words have been spoken, as when we put on a pair of spectacular heels we are aware of the power they yield. Stilettos create a sexy silhouette, as they lift us to a flattering height and lengthen and shape our legs. The kitten heel teases with playfulness and the block heel represents an air of being in control.

From the outrageous and humorous to the simplistic and chic, heels can tell a story and evoke a moment in time, as well as lift our spirits, give us confidence and make a fashion statement. So, when indulging your shoe fetish, remember, there is literally a pair to touch every sole.

History of heels

The evolution of shoes dates back to early civilizations, when heels were worn for practical purposes by both men and women. It is believed that the first instance heels were worn for fashion was when the Italian noblewoman Catherine de Medici walked up the aisle to marry the Duke of Orléans, the future King of France, in 1533. Made in Florence, Italy, the shoes are reputed to have been just 2in (50mm) in height, but they still enabled de Medici to project a more towering physique that befitted her status. The heels were a huge success and began to be worn by all the ladies at court, who associated them with privilege.

The term 'well-heeled' derives from a person in authority or of great wealth.

The development of the high heel took shape from the 1580s onwards, but it was the 'Louis' heel, first created by shoemaker Nicholas Lestage for King Louis XIV of France in around 1660, that become fashionable with women. These heels displayed a concave curve and were commonly between 4 and 6in (100 and 150mm) in height, the reason why, eventually, they fell out of favour.

Another historic French queen who took to wearing heels was Marie Antoinette, who married the future heir to the French throne, Louis XVI, at the tender age of 14. Obsessed with fashion, she had expensive taste and often spent twice her clothing allowance. Some say her lavish spending contributed to the French Revolution, as it incited public discontent. High heels were regarded as a sign of extravagance during this turbulent time and anyone who wore them was associated with opulence, so the majority of people avoided heels so as not to appear wealthy. After a mock trial for treason, Marie Antoinette climbed the gallows in a pair of 2in (50mm) heels before she was executed by guillotine in 1793.

In 2012 a pair of Marie Antoinette's shoes came up for sale in an auction of 'French Revolution Era Artifacts' in Toulon. The heels, size 3.5, were in remarkably good condition, with only some fading to the ribbon, and made 14 times their estimate, selling for over 50,000 US dollars.

It wasn't until the mid-nineteenth century, during the reign of Queen Victoria of England, that heels became popular fashion items again. Initially, low heels became customary, but gradually the height increased until eventually heels became so high that it was impossible for a lady to walk in them. One popular style, the 'Barrette' – its name deriving from the bars and buttons that fastened the shoe – typically featured a ridiculously high heel. The Victorians believed the instep arch – emphasized by high heels – to be symbolic of the curves of a woman's figure. Some, however, argued that heels were a 'poisonous hook' that created sexual aggression and arousal in men.

After the death of Queen Victoria in 1901, heels started to come down in height again. Edwardian women adopted a narrow shoe, as this was seen as a sign of good breeding and gentility, usually in the style of a court shoe with a small 'Louis' heel.

Fashion took a back seat during the First World War. When it finally ended, the frivolous, vibrant 1920s appeared with a burst of confidence, colour and exciting new fashions, which included shoes perfectly designed for dancing the night away.

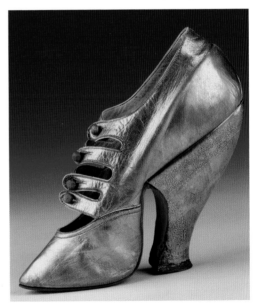

Above: the 'Barrette' shoe, popular in Victorian England, featured a high heel which was believed to be symbolic of the curves of a woman's figure.

Vintage

Retro styling has become in vogue of late, with women seeking out true vintage heels that are either evocative of an era or stand-alone, fabulous, ground-breaking designs. From the 1920s embellished court to the 1970s glam rock platform, there is an abundance of choice, and all of these iconic styles have played an important role in the progression of shoe design through the decades.

The age of jazz

With their fringed dresses, feathered headbands, beaded purses and plenty of rouge, the 1920s 'Flappers' had arrived. Hedonism and liberation were the order of the day for these young and spirited ladies. Having discovered a new-found freedom, they wanted to live life to the full, listen to jazz music, behave in an unacceptable way and dress in a 'boyish' manner.

Some believe that the name 'Flapper' originated because young girls wore unbuckled galoshes that flopped around their legs. A more believable explanation is that they adopted their name after the 1920s movie The Flapper, staring Olive Thomas.

Beginning to change the role of women within society, the Flapper had attitude but was also extremely image conscious, wearing clothes that were in stark contrast to the constricting fashions of the Victorian era. Dresses were waistless and sleeveless, usually in sheer materials and with hemlines that sat just below the knee, which meant that footwear was no longer hidden under masses of petticoats.

Now that shoes were on full view, they played an important role as both a fashion and social statement, but they also needed to be practical and comfortable. One of the most popular styles worn during this decade was the Mary Jane.

Fastened with at least one bar across the instep, these shoes were perfect to wear while dancing the Charleston, as they didn't slip off. Other popular styles worn during the 1920s included the T-bar and the ankle-strap shoes. All, however, displayed straps to keep the shoes in place and all had a heel of around 2in (50mm) in height.

For daywear, shoes would be in plain, dark hues, animal skins or two-tone. Since colour was a resounding feature of the Jazz Age, shoes for the evening were available in a rich variety of hues created from satin and crepe materials. Some were decorated with buckles, bows and trims, while others were emblazoned with embroidery.

Most designs were encrusted with fake jewels, rhinestones and steel beads in the heel area, which tended to showcase the most embellishment.

The Flapper's choice of heels was the perfect representation of their lifestyles, as the shoes were striking, made a statement, oozed confidence and jollity but were also fabulous fun.

Hollywood highlights

The vibrant times of the 1920s quickly came to an end following the American Stock Market Crash in 1929, which caused the Great Depression. A dark cloud was cast and remained throughout this new decade. Unemployment was high, so frivolous spending was out of the question, and the threat of a Second World War was also hanging in the air. So, as respite from the harshness of everyday life, people turned to the silver screen as a form of escapism. The Hollywood idols, dressed in glamorous fashions, projected a happier outlook on life, which was soon adopted by women as they replicated the styles of Greta Gabo, Jean Harlow, Marlene Dietrich and Joan Crawford within their own wardrobes.

Fortunately, shoes didn't suffer greatly during this abstemious period, as glamour was still high on the agenda for stylish ladies. This decade also saw some innovative designs come to the forefront, with French shoe designer Roger Vivier developing the first platform shoe and Italian designer Salvatore Ferragamo creating the wedge heel, in 1936, from cork and wood.

Although there was an extensive variety of shoe styles available throughout the 1930s, which had followed through from the previous decade, it was the high heel that was most in demand because ladies wanted to gain height when wearing their mid-length dresses. The wedge was perfect, as it towered at 5in (127mm) and was also comfortable, due to the solid heel that extended up from the sole.

Dorothy's ruby slippers, worn by Judy Garland in the 1939 film The Wizard of Oz, have become one of the most iconic, treasured and valuable pieces of film memorabilia. One of the five pairs known to exist sold for 2 million US dollars in 2012.

Round-toe pumps, high heels, slip-ons and lace-ups were other shoe designs made fashionable during this era. Black was the prominent colour for daywear, although some women did opt for navy or maroon. Two-tone shoes were also at the height of fashion, but these were very plain with no embellishment. The strappy sandal, which had not made an appearance since the Roman era, became the style to be seen in. Having exposed toes, this elegant shoe was perfect for wearing to evening engagements.

Make do and mend

The eventual outbreak of the Second World War in 1939 resulted in the 1940s being a decade that once again began in a dark place. Women stepped back into their roles within the working environment, filling in while the men were away fighting. Many joined the Women's Land Army, while others worked in munitions factories. The favoured footwear was hard-wearing, practical and comfortable military styles. Restrictions on the use of materials such as leather and rubber also meant that people would 'make do or mend' with the clothes and shoes they already owned. Wastefulness was not an option throughout the war years and everything was expected to last for as long as possible.

The majority of women in Britain were restricted to purchasing just a couple of pairs of shoes each year, but overseas in America rationing was less vigilant and women could buy as many as three pairs. The footwear during this era was plain, with little or no embellishments. Above all, it was designed to be durable.

The USA created a regular ladies' heel height, which was limited to just 1in (25mm).

Shoemakers began to experiment with materials that were more widely available, with reptile skins, mesh, fabric or even straw used as uppers and wood or cork making perfect alternatives to leather for the soles. The main factory of Clarks Shoes in Somerset was closed to make torpedoes. However, they were able to manufacture a unique hinged wooden sole, so they could continue to create essential footwear in their other factories.

Favoured designs were round-toe pumps with a small heel, sandals and court shoes. Dull colours reflected the military styles worn by the working women during the day, with the dominant colours of utility shoes being black and brown. For evening, ladies would dye shoes they already owned in a colour that matched their choice of dress.

Towards the end of the decade when the austere war years had finally come to an end, high fashion began to take centre stage again. The most ground-breaking being Christian Dior's 1947 'New Look', which introduced the hourglass silhouette back into fashion, with fuller-spreading, mid-calf-length skirts and a revisit to the Victorian era with a nipped-in waistline. Heels grew taller, leather was the primary material for shoes' manufacture and the more provocative peep-toe made an appearance. Fashion was back on track with a softer, more romantic feel, so everything about a lady's late-1940s look, including her shoes, was both elegant and feminine.

Fabulous fifties

These post-war years saw a dramatic turn in the progression of shoe design, with many innovative new styles, designs and designers all coming to the forefront. Experimental footwear, such as the 'heel-less' court shoe first created by French shoe designer André Perugia, gave the illusion that the wearer was suspended in the air. Pinet, another French designer, was soon to follow with the same concept, but unfortunately these shoes failed to win popularity and so (pardon the pun) never 'took off'. However, with the austere years of the 1940s a distant memory and the economy on the road to recovery, there were many successful designs that did change the face of fashion in a positive way.

Shoe styles during the 1950s were varied, with women now having a choice of Lucite (Perspex) mules, court shoes, flats, slingbacks and the ubiquitous saddle shoe (Oxfords), which were perfect for wearing with vast skirts when out dancing, as they had very low heels. Closed-fronted shoes became very pointed at the toes and backless mules, known as 'Spring-o-Lators', which possessed a bridge of elastic tape between the ball of the foot and the heel on the insole to keep the shoes in place, became fashionable towards the end of the decade.

The most dramatic ground-breaking shoe design revived during this decade was the stiletto heel. Drawing attention to the leg and calf, this slender heel is documented as being around in the 1930s, but the 'little dagger' (which is how it has come to be known, as stiletto translates to dagger from Italian) has been attributed to iconic French shoe designer Roger Vivier, who was responsible for bringing it back into fashion during the 1950s.

Vivier's most notable commission was a pair of gold kidskin leather heels studded with garnets for Queen Elizabeth II to wear for her coronation in 1953. The upper pattern echoed the fleur-de-lys motif on the St Edward's and Imperial State Crowns.

Often referred to as 'the Fabergé of footwear', Roger Vivier was a sculptural genius when it came to heel design. Aside from the stiletto, he also created the comma heel, pyramid and escargot to name a few. One of the most iconic shoemakers of the twentieth century, his label still lives on and continues to produce stunning creations in shoes.

Swinging sixties

Finally, Britain was back. The economy was booming and the fashion industry was at its height. The 1960s was a decade when freedom of choice ruled and exciting new trends, cultural interests and social scenes were born. The post-war baby boom had created a new 'youthquake' generation, who wanted to break free from the constraints of their elders.

Many shoe designs crossed over from the previous decade, with pointed-toe stilettos and round-toe heeled pumps still being popular. However, with the new mass-produced street-style fashions replacing high-end couture, suddenly the boot became the favoured footwear. Most common for women was the go-go boot, which was worn with the new Mod style of a mini-skirt and tights. Between calf and knee length, these boots could have a shorter kitten heel, a stiletto or a low heel and would possess a round, chiselled or pointed toe. Accentuating a lady's leg, go-go boots worked perfectly with the momentous mini-skirted look.

British fashion designer Mary Quant produced her own version of the man's elastic-sided Chelsea Boot, which had been made famous by pop sensation The Beatles, as part of her footwear range. Entitled 'Quant A Foot', these boots were created from clear plastic over a coloured lining. The heels were moulded with Quant's signature daisy motif, so that when it rained the wearer would leave a trail of daisy footprints behind her after walking in a puddle.

A broad palette of colours was available for shoes, which were often seen in vibrant hues or, following the 'Mondrian' trend, in blocks of colour. The black and white Op Art imagery made popular by the Mod movement was translated onto fashion and, in turn, shoes. Pop Art patterns of swirling psychedelic bright pinks, turquoises and greens also made a welcome appearance.

Designers continued to experiment with materials, looking to historic moments to influence their creations. Pierre Cardin and André Courrèges were inspired by space flight and man's first landing on the moon, and so designed ranges of 'space age' clothing from vinyl, silver fabrics, often featuring large zips. Complementary footwear in the form of boots were added to complete the look of their collections.

Not quite as outrageous and more commonly worn during this decade were plastic shoes – those made out of synthetic materials imitating leather and shiny patent. Such shoes nearly always had a slender kitten or stiletto heel, as the 1960s lady was still conscious of her feminine, but now bold, playful and sexy, image.

Seventies glam rock

An eclectic mix of styles, from flower power hippies to glam rock and the anti-establishment punk movement, all had their time in the limelight in the 1970s. However, the shoe design most synonymous with this era has to be the oversized platform.

Even though the platform has made short appearances throughout the history of shoes – most notably dating as far back as the Ancient Greeks, who wore these heightened shoes to show the importance of characters within the theatre – this giant of a shoe was famously spiralled back into mainstream popularity during the 1970s by the glam rock pop idols. David Bowie, T Rex and Elton John were among those renowned for wearing ridiculously high platforms that complemented their flamboyant images.

A platform is defined as having a thick sole of at least 4in (100mm) under the front part of the foot and it may have various heel designs, including stiletto, wedge and chunky.

Often referred to as 'the disco age', 1970s fashion was all about glitter, sparkle, bell-bottoms and funky shoes. The platform was worn by both men and women for daywear as well as evening. Created from wood, plastic or cork, the sky-high heels came in diverse styles – including knee-high and ankle boots, strappy sandals and lace-up brogues – and many colours – burnt orange and olive green being the staple 1970s hues.

Embellishment also formed part of the decadent 'glam rock' image, so glitter was used unsparingly.

Iconic designer Terry De Havilland is renowned for making the 'disco shoe' and says that shoes are in his psyche. Famous for making Tim Curry's platform shoes for *The Rocky Horror Picture Show* in the 1970s, as well as coloured snakeskin three-tiered wedges worn by the likes of Bianca Jagger, Havilland has become synonymous with creative shoe design and his 1970s platforms are highly prized by those who adore vintage heels.

Although a massive style statement, platforms were not practical footwear, as their height made it difficult to walk. Many people ended up with broken ankles after they had toppled over.

The platform is still a popular shoe design, but it is not quite in the same league as the dizzy heights of those of the glam rock era. The style has become (in most cases) more sensible and easier to walk in. An outlandish heel – or, rather, sole – that was not only the height of fashion but also at its highest should remain 'back in the day' where it belongs, a design that can only ever be associated with the most daring 1970s fashion crazes.

Elton John's cherry-red Dr Marten platform boots (actually stilts and moulded in fibreglass) that he wore when playing the role of the Pinball Wizard in the 1975 film Tommy, measured 54½in (138.5cm) in height.

Eighties power

With big hair and bigger shoulder pads, the 1980s was all about living the power dream. The economy was booming, 'success' was the buzz word and 'Yuppies' (Young Upwardly Mobile Professionals) flaunted their wealth. Image was of the utmost importance and designer labels were branded on just about everything as proof of affluence.

The first ever female Prime Minster, Margaret Thatcher, came to power in Britain, leading the way women should dress if they wanted to infiltrate the male-dominated executive arena. Low-heeled pumps – made popular by Diana, Princess of Wales – were the corporate footwear of choice, in sombre colours to match the black or navy tailored suits that indicated the wearer meant business.

'I understand women because I am a woman. Women love shoes and I love to make women happy. My shoes have done so well over the years because I know what women want and what men dream about.' Beverly Feldman

As the decade progressed, skirts grew shorter and heels became sexier. Slingback or closed courts with pointed toes and slender stiletto heels, became more desirable. Manolo Blahnik's sky-scraper spiked designs were showcased on every catwalk, proving that women could afford expensive designer creations now that they had secured success within the working environment.

Colour, almost regardless of design, was significant from the mid-1980s, as shoes had to match both handbag and tights. Bold fuchsia or electric blue, turquoise, purple, red and fluorescents were the hues to be seen in. Designer Beverly Feldman used eye-catching blocks of clashing colour that present an explosion of vibrancy, while the iconic French designer Charles Jourdan predominantly created one-colour designs that were simple yet technically brilliant, such as his classic fuchsia sandal with its thin-ribbed moulded heel and sole.

Towards the end of the decade gold, pewter and metallic shades were popular, as they matched every outfit colour. As did another firm favourite, the white stiletto, which was worn with skirts, dresses, leggings and, of course, the power suit.

Luxe

Exuberant and majestic designs, conceived from rich materials and adorned with sparkling jewels, showcase luxuriance in a pair of heels. There is no such thing as overdoing the embellishment. In fact, the fancier your footwear the better, because if your shoes dazzle then you will too.

Bling

Fast forward to the twenty-first century and literally anything goes. Of course, there is the must-own fashion style of the season but, in general, ladies have freedom of choice as to which shoe designs to wear. Whether it be the classic court or the Mary Jane, sky-high wedges or stilettos, there is no hard-and-fast rule as to which style a lady should adorn her feet with. However, when it comes to embellishment, there are those ladies who choose to sparkle.

There is no denying 'bling' is in. Heels encrusted with diamanté, rhinestones and faux jewels are everywhere. Some are smothered in glistening stones; others, as in the 1920s, are emblazoned only on the heel area. For the more demure lady, a hint of glimmer in the form of a diamanté buckle, or stones studded around the upper to convey chic elegance, suffices. The sought-after 'bling' effect is usually achieved by the use of Austrian-cut crystals, the most luxurious being by the

'Don't let anyone ever dull your sparkle.'

manufacturer Swarovski. Known for their brilliance and value, Swarovski crystals are faceted lead glass, expertly machine cut and polished to give radiance. Many high-end fashion designers will only use Swarovski crystals in their creations. However, if these sparklers blow the budget, there are other varieties of Austrian crystals used for embellishment, as well as rhinestones and faux jewels. All project the same lush effect and are certain to shine a spotlight on your dazzling shoes when you party the night away.

Fashionista Anna Dello Russo created a range of blingtastic heels for H&M in 2012. Diamanté featured prominently on a pair of black leather ankle-strap sky-scraper sandals. With five thick bands encrusted with bling across the foot and a gold metal buckle on the ankle, these evocative heels are the ultimate bling indulgence.

Shimmering

Wearing heels adorned with glitter and/or sequins is another way to ensure you achieve that shimmering bling effect and they are a popular alternative embellishment to crystals and jewels. Available in an assortment of colours, including multicoloured for a more three-dimensional texture, these light-reflective materials have played an important role in fashion and society for many centuries.

We have always been attracted to shimmering materials. Cavemen would use flakes of mica, a shiny mineral found in granite and rocks, to give cave paintings a glittery sheen. Ancient Egyptians ground up iridescent beetle shells or the natural green crystal malachite and then applied them as cosmetics. In the 1930s, American machinist Henry Ruschmann invented a technique for cutting up large quantities of different coloured plastics, which resulted in him establishing a glitter factory. His slogan was, 'Our glitter covers the world.' Its light-reflecting qualities appealed to shoe designers, ensuring that glitter also covers shoes – although it is now used more tastefully than during the glam rock era of the 1970s. As with other forms of bling, sparkling glitter can be found on every style in a multitude of colours, either completely covering the shoe or used more sparingly to enhance the heels. A useful option for glitzing up any look, glitter heels shouldn't be reserved for eveningwear. When worn with any colour-pop clothing, from fluorescents to jewel-bright shades, glitter shoes can make an equally dazzling daywear statement.

Sequins are a similar form of embellishment, as they, too, reflect the light and sparkle. Originally referred to as 'spangles', they were made of metal and were used in ancient times to adorn clothing, their presence signifying the status of the wearer. The word 'sequin' derives from the Arabic 'sikka', which translates into coins, as in the Mediterranean and the Middle East it was customary to sew coins onto traditional costumes as a way of displaying wealth.

'Sequins' are no longer made of metal but, instead, are plastic, round, shiny discs in metallic shades. The days of using them to display wealth have long disappeared, as now sequins can be found adorning both high-end designer and high-street shoes. So, whether it is glistening glitter or sumptuous sequins that you choose to highlight your heels, there is no doubt that you will be the belle of the ball as the play of light they create reflects your inner sparkle and sense of style.

A new breed of avant-garde shoe designers has emerged with a mission to create unique heels that make a strong statement and are often one-off designs. Every combination of material, embellishment and heel type is possible – there are literally no boundaries. Some stick to more traditional designs, while others think outside the box, enticing us with eccentric, exuberant shoes. Wearing these spectacular heels will ensure that you stand out from the crowd, but it will also pay homage to the talented designers who have taken shoe sculpture to a greater level by creating outstanding, lavish footwear that only the fashion-forward can carry off with confidence.

Award-winning Milly J's Shoes' unique creations are worn by many celebrities and have also had the prestigious honour of being showcased at the Northampton Shoe Museum in an exclusive exhibition. Milly J's impressive heels are renowned for being theatrical and eclectic with a blast of eccentricity. Touching the hearts of all who desire originality, these quirky, unconventional heels are coveted by women who understand that idiosyncrasy is paramount when it comes to commanding uniqueness through your choice of shoes. The Scorpio Queen heels, which represent the zodiac sign, harness determination, power, magneticism, force and excitement, and were the first 'Art to Wear' Mary Jane designs that she created. These decadent shoes, painted with gold leaf for its magnetic appeal, display real king scorpions as ornamentation along the outside of each shoe, which were applied using taxidermy techniques. For a complementary softer edge,

handcrafted flower bouquets adorn the toes and black lace trim is used in the heel area. Not for the faint-hearted, these ambitious heels really do elevate the wearer to a higher status.

Milly J is not the only designer to take the humble shoe and transform it into a breathtaking form with unique and unusual techniques. Others who have applied just as astonishing decorative pieces to their shoes include French designer Mai Lamore, who used gold, onyx and agate in the form of a bee to add a touch of class to her rose shoes, and L J Couture, whose Daisy heels are richly embellished with individually applied crystals, so that no two pairs are identical.

Innovation

Over past decades designers have excelled at continually testing the boundaries in search of exciting and fresh ideas to innovate shoe design, challenging every part from heel to toe. Footwear has taken on a host of diverse forms, which have all contributed to the shoe now being viewed as such an important part of fashion history.

In the twenty-first century, many of the original designs are still in vogue, with the 1930s wedge and 1950s stiletto being staples in every woman's wardrobe. However, contemporary designers have taken these historic heel styles and added their own innovative twist to create an even more alluring visual treat.

Back in 1937, French shoe designer André Perugia revealed his latest creation, a 'heel-less' sky-high shoe. Defying gravity, these striking red shoes with gold platform soles were entitled Trompe L'Oeil (fool the eye). Perugia's creations didn't prove popular with the masses at the time, but fast-forward to the present and the 'heel-less' shoe is a popular fashion choice. Antonio Berardi started his 'heel-less' shoe trend in the summer of 2008, when Victoria Beckham is said to have purchased a pair of his sandals; she was also photographed wearing 'heel-less' thigh-high PVC boots by Berardi at her perfume launch in New York. When Lady Gaga donned a pair of towering, embellished 'heel-less' shoes it catapulted their creator, Japanese designer Noritaka Tatehana,

into stardom. The no-heel design can now be found everywhere, from high end to high street, but this 'innovation' was really the work of Perugia more than 70 years ago and is just another example of a historic design being reworked.

The 'invisible heel' was prolific in a range created by Maison Martin Margiela for a collaboration with H&M stores in 2012. Both pump shoe styles and boots exhibited a Perspex transparent wedge heel, which gave the effect of the shoe being suspended in the air as if it is floating. Made of leather, the boots came in both ankle and knee-high versions in black and brown, while the pumps were available in nude or patent black or red. This ground-breaking style attracted much attention from shoe lovers and had the added advantage of being comfortable and easy to walk in.

There have been countless other innovations when it comes to shoe design. Some heels represent flower stems; others are fashioned into circular, triangular or square shapes. The famous Light Orb shoes by Chanel have actual light bulbs as heels, which light up. Alexander McQueen created shoes with two heels, which were worn by Lady Gaga, and there are even shoes that have faux-lipsticks for heels.

'I design like an architect. It is a beautiful, distinctive art, and shoes are like the foundations.' Jimmy Choo

Designer

For discerning feet, only the best shoes will do and there are none more desirable than those with a high-end designer label attached. Jimmy Choo, Christian Louboutin, Christian Dior and Manolo Blahnik are just a handful of the names associated with beautiful, alluring heels – the crème de la crème of footwear. Granted, these shoes don't come cheap, but when they make the wearer feel like a million dollars, money doesn't come into it. With thousands of styles and designs, it is impossible to look at them all, but when you want to buy quality, then these designer offerings always stand the test of time.

One of the most notable and immediately recognizable of all designer heels has to be those created by French designer Christian Louboutin.

His luxury footwear, with its trademark lipstick-red lacquered soles, are renowned for their distinctive styling and universally adored by ladies around the world. His shoes are sexy, alluring and sultry. Usually with a slender, high stiletto but very occasionally a lower heel, they are the ultimate style statement when it comes to showing off your inner designer diva.

Christian Dior is another name instantly identified with elegant shoes that possess panache. Dior's first shoe line was launched in 1953 with the help of Roger Vivier. Renowned as Dior's star shoemaker, Vivier created opulent heels adorned with lace, pearls, jewels, appliqué and silk. The two collaborated by ensuring that the shoes complemented Dior's fashion lines and vice versa.

'I like women with style to wear my shoes.'

Manolo Blahnik

'The shiny red colour of the soles has no function other than to identify to the public that they are mine. I selected the colour because it is engaging, flirtatious, memorable and the colour of passion.'

Christian Louboutin

One of the most commendable names in fashion, Christian Dior produces shoes with an enduring and timeless appeal. They come in a variety of designs, both traditional and unusual, and are always highly prized. One of the most innovative designs was the couture limited-edition gladiator shoe with a cut-out platform wedge in rich purple suede with gold metal trim.

There are literally hundreds of talented high-end designers whose delectable shoes are coveted by shoe lovers the world over. British designer, Nicholas Kirkwood is one such example. His visionary, elaborate and outlandish designs include miniature disco balls inserted into platforms and heels resembling dripping wax, while his famous collaboration with 1980s American graffiti artist Keith Haring, produced a feast of delicious graphic heels.

Charlotte Olympia, Alaïa, Sergio Rossi and Alexander McQueen are other well-respected shoe designers who are creating some of the most eloquent and exciting designs in footwear today, all of which are eagerly snapped up by those who appreciate high-end artistry.

Architecture meets fashion:
these stunners are the epitome of true luxury.

Lavish materials

Fine fabrics such as luxurious satin, silks and velvets are among the richest materials for making sexy and seductive shoes that are pure luxury to wear. The finest quality leather, suede, crocodile and snakeskin are also enticing. All conventional materials that have been used for the art of shoemaking for decades and even centuries, they are still considered to be the best indicator for distinguishing between cheap or expensive shoes.

Patent leather is also traditionally a sign of a well-made pair of shoes. Originally, the unique high-gloss finish was achieved by polishing layers of linseed oil, whale oil or horse grease onto the quality-grade leather. Today every type of leather is used and it is treated with chemicals and finally lacquered to achieve the desired patent look.

Lace has always been considered an opulent material and is often found adorning shoes. Whether covering the main body or used as a trimming, this delicate material instills femininity to the shoes it graces. Decorative embroidery sewn with silk thread is also recognized as an exuberant form of ornamentation and gives shoes a sense of richness, especially if inset with sequins and beads.

There are many other materials used for shoe design today that are considered worthy of high-end status if worked by a well-known designer or handcrafted with skill. Wood, Perspex and Melflex plastic, which is used by the brand Melissa Shoes, are all sustainable style and are more contemporary, thus appealing to those looking for alternatives to traditional materials.

Mounted on a cherry-wood plinth, the decadent Edwardiana shoe sculpture by Milly J's Shoes (see below) showcases how modern materials, when combined, can create a classy look, especially when worked to achieve a decorous style as here. Delicately wrapped in gilded skeleton leaves with a twisted silk cord binding, these platform killer heels are coloured with subtle Edwardian brass and peacock-blue hues, with a real peacock feather proudly displayed on the back to add the final finishing touch to the lavish decoration.

Famous

'I did not have three thousand pairs of shoes, I had one thousand and sixty.' Imelda Marcos

Many heels, over the course of time, have found themselves in the spotlight because they have been worn by someone iconic or have been featured on the silver screen. Other shoes are thrust into the limelight simply because of their outrageous price tag or because their design is bordering on the edge of bizarre. Stars in their own right, these heels always grab the public's attention, as they are just as A-list as the rich and famous who choose to own and wear them.

The most prestigious embellished heels that money can buy have been designed by British jeweller Christopher Michael Shellis for the House of Borgezie. Handcrafted from solid gold, they are encrusted with over 2,200 brilliant cut diamonds, which total 30 carats and come in with a price tag of £140,000 ($210,000).

Yes, diamonds are renowned for being a 'girl's best friend', but this exuberantly priced pair is unlikely to be snapped up by everyday shoe-loving fashionistas – even if their pockets allowed – as who would dare to wear in the event that they could be ruined or, even worse, stolen from right under their feet.

Vivienne Westwood's Super Elevated Gilles

Supermodel Naomi Campbell is famous for toppling over on the catwalk when wearing a pair of Westwood's blue mock-croc 'Super Elevated Gilles' in 1993 (see the shoes in green, right).

Queen Victoria's wedding shoes (1840)

The white satin flat shoes trimmed with bands of ribbon were created by Gundry & Sons for Queen Victoria to wear on her wedding day to Prince Albert. Long ribbon ties fastened around the ankles to hold the shoes in place.

Marilyn Monroe, *The Seven Year Itch* (1955)

Salvatore Ferragamo designed the white strappy sandals worn by actress Marilyn Monroe in the iconic scene from the film *The Seven Year Itch*, where she stood over the subway ventilation grate with her dress billowing up around her legs.

Alexander McQueen's 'Armadillo' heels

Famously worn by pop icon Lady Gaga in her 'Bad Romance' video, these hoof-like heels had a 10in (255mm) stiletto and were so crazy that they have become worldwide icons.

Tribal

Urban tribal trends are continually in demand by fashionistas. Bold, bright colours, beading, and animal and Aztec prints dominate, as this exotic yet almost fierce and savage style is welcomed by those wanting to add an earthy, naturalistic edge to their look. Inspired by ethnic cultures and infused with Western design, every shoe form has at some point paid homage to the vibrancy of tribal life and style.

Leopard

One of the most prolific examples of the tribal trend is leopard print, which is now considered a classic and appears as ornamentation on all manner of fashion items. At some stage, every shoe shape and style has been adorned with leopard print, sometimes combined with bold colours but mostly as a stand-alone pattern.

Nowadays, faux-fur is used to create the animal-print effect, but historically real animal skins have played a significant role when it comes to adornment. At one time it was believed that animal skins had magical powers that amplified spiritual acumen, and in the early twentieth century fur was regarded as a symbol of wealth and status. In modern times we no longer look at these prints as possessing precious qualities, although they are still considered to be bold and powerful designs.

Wearing leopard print has, at times, been deemed tacky and cheap, but today this audacious print is regarded as chic and stylish if worn in a tasteful manner. Leopard print is sexy, as it brings out the animal instincts of the wearer. It is strong and daring, as only those with confidence can carry it off with ease and panache. It is also playful, fun and flirtatious, ensuring that this print will for ever remain expressive of sartorial style.

'My weakness is wearing too much leopard print.'

Jackie Collins

'Zebra print can bring out your wild side.'

Another of the hottest trends around is zebra print. The monochrome stripes are an appealing option for those who wish to appear classic and chic but also want to demonstrate their daring side. Designer Jimmy Choo achieved this balance perfectly when he incorporated zebra-print heels into his exclusive collection for H&M stores in 2009. The peep-toe sandal with a skinny stiletto heel was a vision of zebra, studs and crystals, showcasing how imitation-animal skins can successfully deliver femininity and sophistication.

Classic zebra is, of course, black and white, but there are also a variety of colours that are often incorporated into this print. Hot pinks, brilliant blues, vivid greens and orange, or even silver, can form the ground for the black stripes, with these bold, contemporary colourways delivering a quirky and fanciful alternative to the traditional print.

Wearing animal print as an accent will guarantee that it won't cheapen or overpower an ensemble. This is easily achieved through shoes. A neutral black outfit will instantly be enhanced when a pair of striking monochrome zebra-print heels are worn as a finishing touch. They are also the ultimate party shoe, especially when flaunting a dash of bling.

Zebra-print is a timeless classic that commands much respect. It can add an essence of glamour with the overall result being very cosmopolitan.

Zebra

Snakeskin

With its broad spectrum of patterns, exotic snakeskin has always been looked upon as an enduring trend in the fashion world, especially in shoe design and for other leather goods. From the elaborate geometric python, the eye of the cobra and the striped sea snake to the more delicate dotted scales of the Karung water snake, these intricate prints are urban classics.

The serpent is a powerful and bold creature, worshipped for centuries around the world for its strength and mysterious 'rebirth' with the shedding of its skin. Each species has a unique and delicate combination of pattern and colour that translates as a work of art when used in fashion.

Genuine snakeskin comes at a price, not only monetary, but also because the snake has to be killed in order for its hide to be used. Although there are those who still choose to opt for genuine snakeskin luxury goods, there are many who will happily wear synthetic leather embossed with scaly replica prints, as they are just as entrancing.

American designer Tom Ford's genuine Anaconda over-the-knee boots with gold-tipped stiletto heel, made a fierce fashion statement when sported by A-listers such as singers Rihanna and Brandy and reality star Khloe Kardashian.

Big and bold python is a daring print that oozes confidence. Karung is more subtle with an almost lizard-like texture, suiting those who prefer a hint of snake style that isn't too imposing. Generally, snakeskin is tones of brown or black against a lighter complementing ground, but the print can also be created in all colours of the rainbow for a fun and striking interpretation. A versatile print that can be found on every shoe style, snakeskin is one of the staples that works well during the day as a sophisticated classic and is perfect for giving an evening ensemble a mysterious, sultry edge.

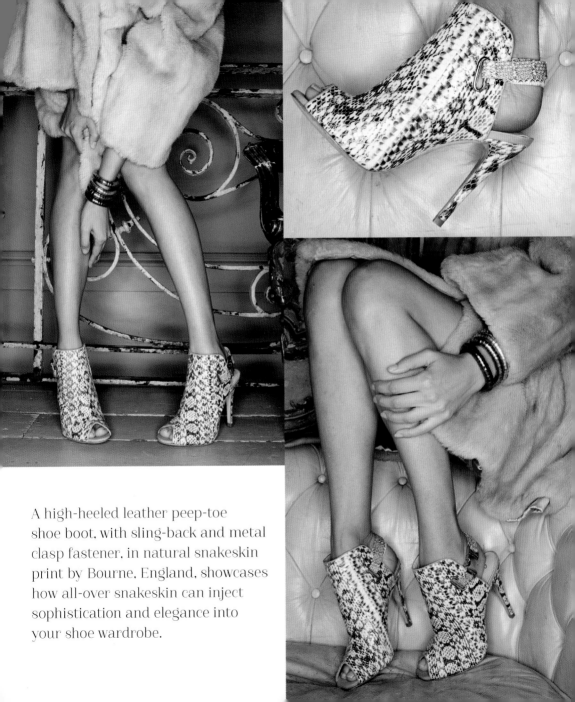

A high-heeled leather peep-toe shoe boot, with sling-back and metal clasp fastener, in natural snakeskin print by Bourne, England, showcases how all-over snakeskin can inject sophistication and elegance into your shoe wardrobe.

Beading

Ethnic beading is synonymous with tribal-inspired designs, as it is the epitome of African and Asian style. The vibrant and natural hues of beadwork reflects the colour and flamboyance of the music, dance and fashions of these cultures. Versatile and expressive, it is a vivacious three-dimensional form of decoration when applied to shoe styles.

Originally prestigious trade items between Africa and Europe, beads were used as currency, as adornments for the body and clothing, to make jewellery and as objects of art. They could be exchanged for services and slaves, which is why they are often referred to as slave beads. Glass beads made in Europe were particularly desirable in Africa, especially those with fine decoration, such as millefiori. Early beads were made from natural materials, such as bone, wood and even eggshell, which were presented to a woman in her dowry. Beads are still created from natural products, such as wood, seeds or coral, and glass remains popular, along with plastic and metal.

Contemporary shoes tend to be embellished with wood or plastic beading, either hung in strings from the ankle area to flow onto the top of the foot, as illustrated by Burberry in their Prorsum collection of 2012, or applied to areas of the shoe for a hint of tribal style. For more daring ladies, heels that are entirely covered with tiny coloured beads arranged into flowing geometric patterns offer the ultimate tribal tribute, such as the Hoxton beaded platforms by Miss KG Kurt Geiger, which showcase a detailed tapestry of tiny beads.

An earthy, naturalistic look, tribal beading is perfect for the summer, as it suggests sunshine, warmth and a free spirit. Sandals are the classic choice for delivering a touch of tribal style, although beaded embellishment can be just as striking on the court shoe or slingback. An enduring trend that is hotly anticipated every year, this look is not only about wearing high fashion, but also about transporting you to faraway lands where history and culture is celebrated through the use of beads.

The South African Zulu tribes have a code for their beads. Blue, supposedly, enhances fertility, black is for age and wisdom, gold indicates a long life, yellow is for the high-ranking and red is used for special ceremonies.

Ethnic prints

If you are looking to expose your inner extrovert, then heels in loud and vivacious patterns are ideal. Ethnic and tribal prints are visions of vibrancy, and include a diverse range of strong, oversized graphics with geometric styling and clashing colours.

Although we generalize by lumping these prints into categories, such as ethnic and tribal, each one of them is very different, originating from all corners of the globe and being created using specific techniques. The up-and-down Ikat print, with its distinctive bleeding-dye effect, has been created all over the world. The Ganado pattern of diamonds, crosses and bands began life in the Navajo Nation in the USA, as did the Chinle, which is made up of bands of stripes and geometric shapes. Dutch Wax, as its name suggests, originates from the Netherlands, where the Indonesian technique of wax-resistant dyeing, known as batik, was adopted in order to create fabric for the African market. Batik is a popular African and Southeast Asian print.

The Western market has adapted these traditional prints by adding contemporary twists, so the patterns are now loosely associated with their origins but still retain a native vibe. Swirls and bands of colour, geometric and abstract shapes and symbolism all feature. When transferred onto a shoe form, these bold patterns create an assertive visual treat.

Ikat and graphic patterns are the most prolific found on footwear, as they are wearable prints that work well during the spring and summer seasons; if displaying earthy, darker hues, they can also look striking as eveningwear. Much like beading, these evocative prints can be found covering the entire shoe or enhancing specific areas. A shoe with a wedge heel, for instance, can make more visual impact if it is just the wedge part that carries the graphic print.

The one thing that all the variations of prints have in common is that they are distinctive, bold, native patterns that come in a plethora of colours and designs, which can be easily incorporated into your personal shoe style.

A feast of exoticism, these traditional prints are perfect for making a powerful statement.

Exuberant tribal tints cheer up a dreary day, have the ability to put a smile on your face and let people know you are not afraid to experiment with clashing hues.

Vivid jewel tones are renowned for being associated with tribal designs. These luscious colours of the rainbow feature shades of turquoise, jade green, cobalt blue, bright orange and pink, red and yellow all coming together in a cluster of vibrancy. Earthy naturalistic hues are also a tribal trait, with shades of rustic brown, olive green, burnt orange and warm burgundy being typical.

All of these colours would have had a certain significance when worn within a particular native tribal environment, although most meanings vary. For some Native American tribes yellow signifies dawn and sunshine, but if worn as face paint it is associated with death and mourning. Green is a representation of plants, but when it is used as face paint under the eyes, it is believed to empower the wearer with night vision. This gives a fascinating insight into the importance of colour within tribal cultures.

For the purpose of westernized contemporary prints, colours don't have the same meaning. They are simply delightful hues that attract the eye, complement an outfit or reflect your mood at a given time. So don't be concerned if your vivid shoes, mainly sporting yellow shades, are giving off the impression of mourning, because as you are probably already aware, this glorious colour is more associated with having a sunny outlook on life.

Another option to consider is shiny metallic, which instantly takes the tribal trend to a more glitzy and sparkly place. Shades of silver, bronze, pewter or gold add richness to any design and are the ideal neutral base colours for a shoe that is adorned with graphic prints or beading, as it can easily make the transition from day into night.

Native colours are fun, funky and fabulously flirtatious. An explosion of colour for the feet, these tribal trends are here to stay, so embrace them and wear your shoes with pride.

Tribal colours

Classic

The sophisticated pump, elegant sandal and obligatory boots are all timeless, classic designs that should be found in every woman's shoe wardrobe. Stiletto and kitten heels, the wedge, chunky platform and the single sole all form the foundations, with the main body of the shoe being conservative for that time-honoured look. Footwear staples, these shoes will never date, ensuring that you always have a pair to fit every occasion.

Court shoe

There are times when your heels need to mean business. They have to exude confidence and professionalism, but also remain feminine, elegant and stylish. For centuries, height has been associated with power; anyone of any importance would don sky-high heels, towering over those of lesser standing. Back in the 1980s (see page 24), power within the workplace prevailed among women, which is why they opted for the sexy yet dominant spiked high heel. There is no denying that women feel more self-assured if we walk

taller, with the stiletto still being a popular style choice for those that want to be taken seriously.

The mid-heel is another favourite among working women. Usually only 2½in (64mm) in height, it is not as tall as the stiletto and definitely not as alluring, but this mini heel still portrays a chic silhouette and, most importantly, it is comfortable to wear throughout an eight-hour day.

The chunky heel has also become an attractive option for those in the working environment, as it is another comfortable choice. The good, solid heel will keep you well balanced all day, so there is no risk of teetering.

All of these classic heel designs are generally found on the equally classic closed-toe court or pump shoe style, with either a rounded or pointed toe. Ideal for the working woman who wants to project a smart, conservative look, the court is a perfect example of simplistic styling, with clean, defined lines that lend the wearer an aura of efficiency and aptitude. The business court shoe tends to be very plain with little or no embellishment, sometimes displaying a two-tone colourway. Patent, mock skin, suede and leather are the most popular materials, with darker hues of black, navy and grey as well as the all-important nude being the accepted business shades.

The court shoe is also a universal choice for the evening, as it can be teamed with either trousers or a skirt. Opt for a pointed-toe stiletto court in gold or silver to add a little more sparkle, or a vibrant hue, such as red, for a rich, sensual look that will showcase your adventurous side.

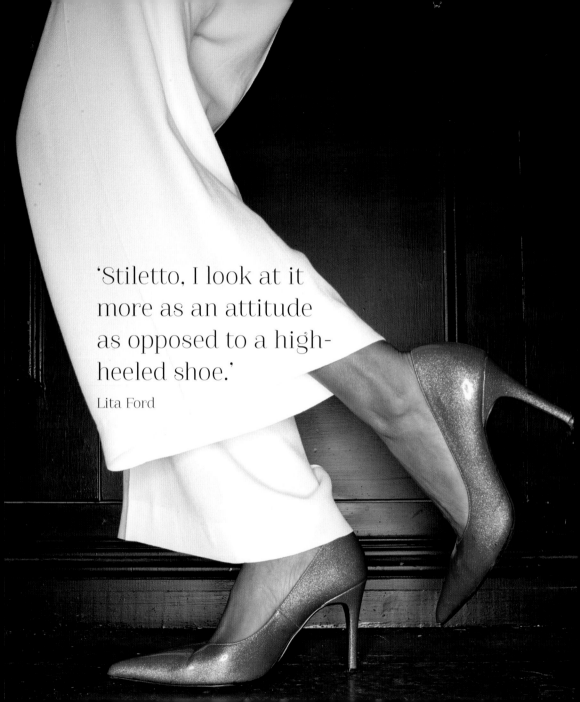

'Stiletto, I look at it more as an attitude as opposed to a high-heeled shoe.'

Lita Ford

Strappy

Whether it is a gladiator or a cut-out, a multi-strap or a cage, sandals of all styles are a must, not only for warm summer days, but also to complete an evening ensemble. Elegant and classy, they shout femininity. With their delicate styling combined with on-trend colours, fabrics and patterns, these classic heels are the mainstay of every stylish lady's shoe collection.

The gladiator design is a modern take on the historic *caliga* worn by the Roman military. Found with both flat and high heels, this style of shoe has exposed toes with a lattice upper pattern that is more openwork than the tighter design of the cage shoe. Multi-strap sandals, as their name suggests, feature straps across the foot, sometimes with an additional ankle strap and always with exposed toes. Cut-out sandals vary in design, depending on the size and shape of the cut-out effect.

Unashamedly seductive, the heeled sandal is a true wardrobe staple. Available in a plethora of designs, colours and patterns, some sandals are simplistic while others are more sculptural compositions. Many shine with rhinestones; others display intricate patterns or animal skins.

For a conventional classic style, then a sandal in neutral colours, such as black, brown or nude, is essential for wearing during the day, with silver or gold being advisable for nocturnal celebrations. These colours will work with any outfit choice.

Many stylish ladies own several pairs of sandals in various colours and designs, as this type of shoe is ideal for almost any occasion. Just as it was back in the 1930s (see page 15), the strappy sandal is still regarded as the ultimate in glamour and elegance, and will ensure that you are party-ready at all times.

'You sold your soul to the devil when you put on your first pair of Jimmy Choo's, I saw it.'

Emily to Andy in The Devil Wears Prada (2006)

'When you walk in mules, you walk a bit differently. It's very sexy to me; you have to get your balance. Egyptian queens would be walking around in these kind of mules of gold and ivory – can you imagine? – click click click … and Madame de Pompadour in her mules, walking around Versailles, click click click … Can you think of anything more exquisite?'

Manolo Blahnik, W magazine

Mule

The name 'mule' was derived from the Latin, *mulleus calceus*, which was a dark red leather ceremonial shoe worn by Roman senators in Ancient Rome. By the eighteenth century the term referred to a high-heeled design that was worn as an indoor shoe.

More recently, in the early twentieth century, the mule was associated with prostitution, so the shoe style was shunned by genteel ladies. However, the glamorous silver-screen star Marilyn Monroe is said to be responsible for changing this attitude by popularizing the mule as a fashion item in the 1950s. A backless shoe, which traditionally has

a closed or partially closed front, the mule has remained acceptable footwear fashion ever since.

As Manolo Blahnik observed in an interview for *W* magazine, the simplistic mule possesses a unique sound when the wearer walks in it, which is so distinctive that you instantly attract attention. It is one of the most basic but adaptable shoe styles. A high-heeled mule is sexy and alluring, while the lower-heeled version is chic and classic. Some women still choose to wear open-toed mules only indoors, with the red or black pom-pom mules being renowned as a classic boudoir look, reinforcing the mule's connotations of sexiness.

Wedge

The wedge is a good, solid heel, which, since its inception in the 1930s, is still very much a classic shoe design. More comfortable than most heels and certainly more sturdy, the wedge is a shoe that should be worn with a confident stride. Be aware, however, that a wedge will render you unable to run – but then, how many stylish women really want to be seen racing along in their heels?

Extremely versatile, the wedge is compatible with almost any outfit, although it is more striking as a daytime shoe, being a bit too chunky and clumpy for eveningwear. Maxi, midi and mini skirts can all be complemented with a wedge shoe, as this type of heel adds height and gives definition to the ankle. Trousers also work well with a wedge, but it is advisable to expose a few inches of the ankle below the hem when wearing tight-fitting skinnies, as the more robust wedge can create a clunky, bottom-heavy silhouette. It may not be the most elegant of shoe designs, but the wedge is perfect for those who want to glam up their daytime look with a pair of eye-catching heels that make more of a comfortable fashion statement than a graceful one.

Despite its lack of elegance, the wedge is still one of the most popular forms of shoes worn by women, as it is aesthetically pleasing and always on-trend. Available in a variety of materials from wood to raffia and cork to synthetic leathers, these sturdy shoes can be found brandishing every pattern and embellishment, as well as being available in each and every plain colour imaginable.

Very much a summer shoe, wedges explode onto the fashion scene every year, all sporting the latest must-have hues and trends. Women everywhere walk tall in their wedges, because from colour pop to monotone and abstract to floral, there is a solid sole to suit every lady's foot.

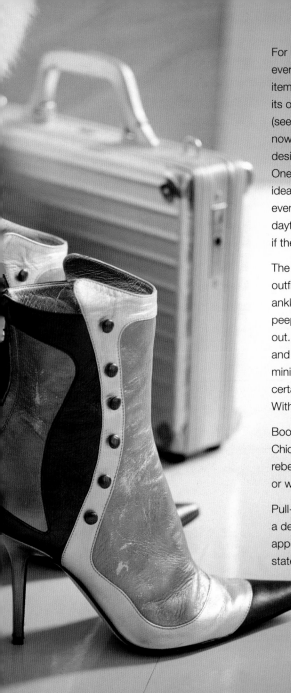

For utilitarian purposes, the boot has been around for ever, and even though it became popular as a fashion item during the nineteenth century, it really came into its own as a widespread trend from the 1960s onwards (see page 20). Ankle, calf, knee-high and thigh boots are now all desirable footwear, available in every colour and design, and suitable for both casual and dressy affairs. One of the key pieces in your shoe wardrobe, boots are ideal with jeans, trousers and skirts, for dressing up an evening ensemble and complementing a smarter daytime outfit. Boots are also deemed sexy, especially if they are knee- or thigh-high with a stiletto heel.

The ankle boot is the most versatile, as it works with all outfits. The shoe boot, which stops at the base of the ankle, has recently made a welcome appearance. A peep-toe version is ideal for the summer or for a night out. Knee-high boots are ideal for wearing over leggings and skinny jeans and look just as amazing with a midi or mini skirt. Thigh-high boots are the most seductive – and certainly not for those with a shy and retiring personality. With a stiletto heel, they are the ultimate in raunchy.

Boots can define the identity of a subculture. The Rock Chic favours studded or spiked boots, suggesting a sexy, rebellious attitude. The Goth is likely to go for a platform or wedge boot, with many buckles and always in black.

Pull-on, lace-up or zip-up boots are, like the court shoe, a desirable classic that can be worn in all seasons. Their appeal lies in their ability to suggest a multitude of style statements, depending on how you wear them.

Boot

Platform

Not reaching the towering heights of the 1970s when the style reigned supreme (see page 23), but certainly high enough to raise a lady a few inches from the ground, the platform sole is a popular choice among the fashion-conscious. Vivienne Westwood created her notorious Super Elevated Gilles for the 1993 Anglomania A/W collection, which resulted in supermodel Naomi Campbell taking a tumble on the catwalk (see page 44). Today the platform sole is a little less dangerous and can be found on a variety of shoe designs.

A platform sole can be either visible or concealed and the heel type can be chunky, a stiletto or a platform wedge. A closed-toe pump or peep-toe slingback are the two main shoe forms that display the power-platform sole with the stiletto heel, creating drama without taking away the feminine silhouette. This style of shoe is not really appropriate for everyday wear, because unless they have a wedge-heel platforms can be difficult to walk in for any length of time. As a result, stiletto platforms make great 'restaurant shoes' (walking from the car to the restaurant), but for a glamorous night out, it advisable to pack a pair of flats for when your platforms get the better of your feet.

These heels are, however, a great way to display your individuality, as they cannot be ignored. Sexy and alluring, platform shoes project confidence as well as instilling a sense of spirit. Have fun with the platform by choosing a design with a quirky print or a touch of luxe in the form of rich embellishments, or stick to one-colour designs for a classic staple that suits every occasion. A dramatic fashion statement, they are not for the faint-hearted but for those ladies who need to be noticed for the shoes that they proudly display upon their feet.

Colour

Striking colours, pastel shades, bold prints and a scattering of florals can all add drama to your footwear, while neutral hues and traditional patterns can make for a demure and classic style. Literally every colour of the rainbow can be found adorning shoes and it is these colour combinations that can reflect your mood, individual flair and personality, as well as bringing out the daring side of your persona.

Vibrant

Vivid hues will not only lift your spirits but will also illuminate your sunnier nature and give you a confident and vivacious outlook on life. There is no better reason to brighten up your look by incorporating a pair of vibrant jewel-coloured heels into the mix.

Colour really does reign supreme when seeking that special something in a pair of heels. No matter whether it is one colour or a variety of clashing hues thrown together, all have the same dramatic effect of being the beacon that gets you noticed.

Single shades as well as colour-block or two-tone designs all deliver a visual feast when adorning shoes. Colour never fails to draw the eye, but it is especially effective when the heel is a combination of numerous vibrant hues that all come together to create a work of art. Delivering a spectacular explosion of colour, such confections embrace the beauty of the hues when amalgamated to create one impressive design.

The use of colour can bring a shoe alive, transport us to faraway lands or simply tell a story, as demonstrated by shoemaker Thea Cadabra's intricate Turquoise Water Lily heel, 2010. Depicting delicate tendrils in textured leathers that twist around the shoe, heel and ankle, this shoe is a new version of Cadabra's Water Lily that was first created in black and pink by the designer in 1978. Inspiration for the original shoe design came from all kinds of sources, including the clothing emporium Biba – the fashion mecca of the era – David Bowie, *The Rocky Horror Picture Show* and the kitsch elements of 1950s style. Cadabra's imaginative creations were often decorated with three-dimensional motifs that would add drama and an element of surprise to delight the wearer. This twenty-first century rework of the original is just as intriguing and fantastical, as it takes you to a world of tropical beauty, where there is a touch of sparkle provided by the rhinestone buckle and the flower stamens fashioned from facetted beads.

'Wearing wonderful
shoes is a truly
uplifting experience.'

Thea Cadabra

Abstract

Decorative abstract patterns in artful shapes that culminate in a burst of colour separate us from reality and stimulate our visual imagination. These dynamic prints inject vitality into footwear, as they capture the aesthetic of tribal and ethnic, graphic and impressionistic prints.

The world of art has always played an important role in fashion, as designers continually seek inspiration from a variety of cultures and artistic disciplines and movements for their creations. It is the interpretations of colour that enthralls, in the enthusiastic ways in which it is translated onto heels in exciting and vibrant palettes.

With a plethora of shoe styles decorated with wondrous, fanciful prints, it can be difficult to choose. Many feature bright jewel colours, some are in subtle pastel shades; others are earthy hues. It is really down to personal choice, and which you feel will best complement your outfit and style.

Inspired by surrealist artist Salvador Dalí, the raffia platform sandal created by Olivia Rubin for Dune, is a great example of how abstract prints can breathe life into any style of shoe. The bold pattern of vivid blue, pink and green is broken up with black accents and interwoven with patent straps. The back of the heel upper (the heel counter) is caged, with an ankle strap for fastening, giving this power platform a softer, more elegant feel.

Shoes themselves are a form of artwork, so it is no wonder that designers often express this within their creations. As already mentioned, Nicholas Kirkwood collaborated with graffiti artist Keith Haring on abstract designs for a range of shoes (see page 43). Another British designer, Charlotte Olympia, designed a capsule collection for American store Neiman Marcus. Olympia's Dolly platforms were painted by the photographer and body artist Boyarde Messenger, with images that payed homage to great artists such as Piet Mondrian, Pablo Picasso and Vincent van Gogh.

In most cases, abstract prints are fun, quirky patterns that lend themselves well to the shoe design, with no particular purpose except to be eye-catching. Adorning your feet with these bold, beautiful and uplifting shoes, is sure to brighten up your day as well as your look.

Neon

Be proud and loud with neon shades, as this acidic pop of colour is a trend that can breathe life into your shoe wardrobe. Fuchsia pink, orange, yellow and lime green illuminate, having the most impact when the clashing hues are styled together.

Step back to the 1980s, when neon was a colour phenomenon (see page 24). Literally anything associated with fashion was produced in these super-bright shades, and that included spandex and even make-up. Inevitably, these blinding hues have made a come-back, but thankfully the contemporary designs are more tasteful and shapely than the neon fashions of 30 years ago.

You do need confidence to carry off this fluoro trend, as it is not a look that will let you take a back seat, but will instantly project you into the limelight. The most stylish way forward is to keep your neon minimal, using well-chosen accessories – which, of course, includes shoes – as a way of accenting your look.

If you feel brave, then opt for single-colour heels in a dazzling shade, maybe teamed with equally dazzling but clashing pop socks or tights for the ultimate fashion-forward look. If you are a little more cautious, then choose a flash of neon in the form of a pair of killer heels, which are either one colour or harmoniously display a few electric hues, and wear them with neutral clothing.

This fashion fad won't be around for ever, but while neon flourishes it is worth experimenting with these animated colours to add depth and excitement to your look.

Be bold: a fabulous pair of neon heels will electrify your style in a flash, as there is definitely nothing understated about this fashion craze.

Pastel

Delicious, delicate pastels, in baby pinks and blues, mint greens and lavenders, are a stark contrast to the illuminating neon hues. These subtle shades possess a genteel, ladylike quality, as they are soft, muted tones that are lighter in appearance and gentler on the eye. The ideal spring/summer wardrobe staple, mouthwatering sorbet-coloured pastels radiate romance and are perfect for wearing on idyllic days in the sun.

However, try not to overdo these sickly ice-cream shades by wearing all-over pastel. Neutral navy, brown, black and white are all colours that will complement your pretty pastel heels. Alternatively, match your shoes with a specific piece from your chosen outfit. If you are wearing a lemon-yellow top, for example, choose an identical shade for your footwear, as this will give your look an overall sense of balance.

The pastel vibe is easily achieved when wearing soft-coloured skinny jeans, a short summer dress or even shorts. The shoes will inject an ethereal flair, especially if they are single-coloured pumps or strappy sandals with a kitten or stiletto heel. For a dramatic impact, choose chunky wedge or platform heels in a combination of pastel hues, as they will take away the feminine silhouette and funk up this otherwise dreamy look.

Colour-blocking pastels is a great way to add a new dimension, and there are plenty of heels around sporting confident combinations: blue with mint green, yellow with cupcake pink, or even orange with lilac. There are no set rules, so if you are feeling comfortable with your colour compositions, why not go a step further and inject a brighter jewel hue into the mix – just make sure that it does not contrast too sharply with your pastels.

You can be as daring or as cautious as you want to be with a pastel palette, but try to steer clear from overdoing the style. Mix and match shades, highlight with accents or experiment with colour blocking to get the desired stylish look. Most of all, have fun with your ice-cream pastels and ensure that the end result is sweet and chic.

Two-tone

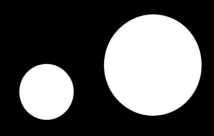

More than 50 years ago in 1957, French fashion designer Coco Chanel first designed her iconic two-tone slingback slipper in beige with a black toe-tip. It is believed that Chanel was inspired by the black leather toes of the shoes worn by the male staff on the Duke of Westminster's yacht, and copied the idea for her own ground-breaking ladies' shoe design. Today the two-tone Chanel shoe is regarded as a timeless classic, with the beige and black colourway being a style choice in a league of its own.

As with any innovative and successful creation, others follow suit and today there are numerous two-tone shoes to choose from. Some are very much in the Chanel style with a contrasting toe-tip, while others feature variations of the design.

For a classic sophisticated look, the two-tone shoe cannot be beaten. It is the ideal choice to impress in a business environment, especially in neutral hues of black, navy, beige, nude or white.

These conventionally coloured shoes can also look amazing if worn with a more on-trend outfit. Black and white pointed-toe courts suddenly add a dash of funk when worn with a pair of black and white animal-skin trousers, which transform these classic designs into party-ready heels.

Revered and adored since its inception, the two-tone shoe has become a true staple thanks to its chic design that complements so many outfits and works for every occasion. The Chanel original has evolved over the decades, with designers making their own interpretations of both the colour combinations and the block designs. However, the two-tone concept is still very much as it sounds – two colours on a shoe that deliver a striking and chic effect.

'A woman with good shoes is never ugly. They are the last touch of elegance.'
Coco Chanel

Floral

A bouquet of blooming floral tributes emblazoned across high-heeled shoes has become a hot trend of late, inviting ladies to embrace their inner chintz. This cute, kitsch look can be found enriching every form of female footwear in an assortment of styles, designs, colourways and embellishments.

Some floral inspirations completely cover the shoe, while others feature subtle sprays or dainty sprigs. Many are influenced by vintage or historic designs, while some heels present a less fussy, simplistic contemporary style. Wearing full-on floral shoes can seem daunting, especially if you have never considered yourself a flowery girly girl, so there is the option to dip your toe (so to speak) into a shoe that is gently enhanced with flowers or one that has an understated pattern that isn't so imposing.

Shoe designer and fashion brand Irregular Choice often feature floral motifs within their creations, which they cleverly blend with complementary patterns, colours and embellishments for a unique and striking balance. Their Stick of Rock heels showcase a green floral print with another classic summer-appropriate fabric, gingham check. A multicoloured metallic bow, topped with a red Perspex double heart and clear arrow decoration, adorns the toe area. A detachable chain of charms on the ankle and a green-tinged engraved heel with a red tip add the finishing touches to this innovative design. A super summer style, this is one of the many pairs of Irregular Choice heels that celebrate and display florals in a flamboyant and funky manner.

Metallic

The molten-hot colours of gold, silver and bronze are all winners when it comes to dazzling in a pair of shining metallic heels. Radiant and chic, these lustrous metal finishes are ideal for those wishing to channel their inner glamour girl.

Heels in traditional metallic hues can easily stand in the place of your neutral ones, as they go with absolutely anything. Silver is one of the most popular metallic hues, especially when worn with black or colours with cool undertones, while gold, bronze and pewter bring earthy shades alive. These gleaming, lusty finishes make willing companions for eveningwear, as they project a charismatic glitzy style, but there is no reason why they can't also be worn during the day. Team them with denim or dark hues and wear them in the form of strappy sandals in the summer or even, if you are daring enough, metallic boots, which will ensure your look has the 'wow' factor.

Aside from the neutral shades, there are also metallic heels in an array of amazing colours, such as hot pink, purples, blues and greens. These heels are too shimmery for daywear, so should be reserved for sparkling evenings out on the town. They also need to be the main focal point of your outfit and are best paired with complementary or toned-down colours.

Metallic finishes vary from the distressed and cracked, which give a more subtle and muted effect, to the highly polished and chrome. Some

of the more vibrant metallic heels sparkle with sequins, so these should be considered as your special party shoes for when you want to shine.

If the all-over metallic shoe feels too daring, then why not try heels that have accents of this trend? There is a wealth of less imposing designs that feature metallic only on the heel, sole or toe-tip.

High-impact, mesmerizing metallic heels will add pizzazz to your wardrobe and evoke shoe envy among those who haven't yet mastered the art of showcasing this hot, sexy trend on their feet.

Dare

Some shoe obsessive's steer clear of conventional heel designs, preferring to adorn their feet in breathtaking styles that only the extrovert dares to wear. This could be due to individual taste or an interest in a specific style, but many choose outlandish designs because they form part of a subculture. Whatever the reason, these spectacular shoes are just as dynamic, inspiring and awesome as your everyday heels. The only difference is that they are more jaw-droppingly outrageous, impressing those whose guilty pleasure is having a die-hard shoe fetish.

'Shoes are sexy.
I mean, everything
has to be sexy. That's
what my job is.'

Vivienne Westwood

Fetish

Fetish culture is provocative, erotic and, in some cases, extreme. Stiletto-heeled shoes and boots created from materials such as latex, leather, rubber, PVC and spandex are associated with this dominant scene. Black and red are the prime colours, and laces and buckles, zips and straps are all key accessories.

True fetish wear is not practical for everyday, as it is considered more akin to costuming and is generally kept behind closed doors. Many fashion designers, however, have taken elements of this subculture and incorporated them into their designs, creating fetish footwear that is more wearable for those in the mainstream.

British designer Vivienne Westwood is probably the most renowned for incorporating fetish-inspired looks into her creations. In the 1970s, together with her former partner, Sex Pistols creator Malcolm McLaren, she designed a range of seditionary punk clothing, which featured bondage trousers that connected the wearer's legs with straps. Having changed the name of their shop on London's Kings Road to Sex in 1974, Westwood and McLaren concentrated on their evocative and sexually crude streetwear designs, which became synonymous with the brand.

Even today Westwood's designs, especially shoes, have a distinct nod to fetishism, with extreme heels that empower the wearer and evoke sexuality by transporting us into a world where ordinary just isn't enough. Some of her iconic designs include the knee-high Pirate Boot, first produced in 1981, and the Canvas Bondage Boot, with concealed lacing, visible buckles and moulded animal toes, from the S/S 2002 Nymphs collection.

'Women's fashion is a
subtle form of bondage.
It's men's way of binding
them. We put them in
these tight, high-heeled
shoes, we make them wear
these tight clothes and we
say they look sexy. But
they're actually tied up.'

David Duchovny

Flirty

'High heels are pride and privilege, the passkey to decadence.'

Karen Heller

Spruce up your look with some fun and flirty heels. Think saucy and sexy: shoes that will make the boys whistle and the girls giggle. Choose footwear that will be enjoyed, amusing both you, the wearer, and the observer, but also shoes that will be admired by those who appreciate the power that a pair of sassy heels can yield.

It is so important to have fun with your footwear, as shoes can be regarded as an extension of your personality, mood or intentions. Wearing witty heels will definitely make sure that all eyes in the room are on you, and if you are feeling in a flirty mood, then highlight this by donning equally flirtatious shoes.

There are, of course, the usual sexy, towering stilettos in hot, passionate colours, or heels that seduce in more obvious ways. It is more interesting, however, to seek out a pair that blatantly suggests flirtatiousness through their deliberate design.

An ideal pair for making that statement and causing a sexy stir are the elegant black-and-white kid-leather Maid Shoes by Thea Cadabra, as they are the epitome of seductive sauciness. The sculptured heel, created by jewellery designer James Rooke, takes the form of a pair of curvaceous female legs below a pretty pleated vamp that makes up the flounced, decorative white bow on the back of the maid's apron. These cheeky yet innovatively artful French-maid-inspired shoes are exactly what you should be wearing when looking to have some harmless flirty fun.

Burlesque

The seduction of burlesque is all about the tease. Flirtatious and inviting, this dazzling fashion trend takes its lead from a provocative art form, which incorporates vintage glamour, corsets, feathers and sexy killer heels.

The burlesque style originates from the amusing theatrical parody, which is acted out by attractive scantily clad women. Historically this cabaret was a form of entertainment for the lower classes, by making fun of serious works, such as plays and operas, and the social habits of the upper classes. Today neo-burlesque is a cabaret of dancing, comedy, striptease and fetish acts, along with music, circus and literary performances that are meant to entice and excite the audience.

Incorporating burlesque fashions into your style is easily achieved, as this is a very feminine and varied look. Sky-high stilettos embellished with showy sequins, feathers, satins and silks are a must, as they achieve that alluring sense of suggestiveness. Vintage styles, such as the 1950s pencil skirt, rockabilly and the golden age of Hollywood, all fit nicely into this glamorous fashion culture. However, if you are more daring, then think Moulin Rouge, lingerie and the corset – although these garments should be reserved for attending burlesque clubs, rather than wearing them on a daily basis.

Burlesque is all about, sex, seduction and the *femme fatale*. It is showy, extrovert and glitzy, so when adopting this style ensure that you are dressed to the nines, wearing heels that are as provocative, sensual and suggestive as you dare.

Boudoir

Literally meaning a room to sulk in (from the French *bouder*, to sulk), the word boudoir refers to a lady's private bedroom or dressing room, usually found next to the main bedroom. It is also commonly used to describe a sexy and seductive style.

Boudoir shoes were originally low-heeled pumps created from satin and silk with tulle bows as decoration. Today these shoes can be far more daring in both height and design. Varying from cutesy pom-pom, feather or fur kitten-heeled peep-toe mules to sexy high-heeled stilettos, your boudoir heels are whatever you wish them to be, as long as they are able to seduce.

The whole point of boudoir shoes is to reserve them for the bedroom. These heels should be provocative, sexy and alluring. They are meant to entice and excite your lover by awakening their sexuality in a classy and sophisticated way. Boudoir shoes should also be feminine and ladylike, as they are flirtatious heels that reflect your womanly characteristics.

Boudoir shoes are often referred to as lingerie for the feet, and shoe designer Thea Cadabra created a pair of heels that perfectly embodies this concept. The Suspender Shoe, which first made an appearance in 1978, is a unique take on the classic boudoir look. A provocative pair of two-tone shoes, they display black suspender

straps as the main focus over the top of the foot and have a 4½in (114mm) heel, which adds even more sensual appeal. Originally, Cadabra designed these shoes to complement a leather mini skirt, which had pink ribbon lacing on the sides, and wore them with seamed stockings to a party. Today they form part of her Boudoir Collection, which is handcrafted in a small artisanal factory in Italy.

Edgy

Wearing unusual heels doesn't have to limit you to the most outrageous designs, it could simply be heels that have an appealing 'edge', which makes them a little out of the ordinary compared with conventional shoe styles. The structure, the embellishment or even the material the heels are made from can add a unique twist to a pair of shoes, and it is this that captivates the wearer and grabs the attention of others.

Melissa Shoes for Vivienne Westwood are a prime example of how you can inject a little uniqueness into your footwear without being too avant-garde. These eco-plastic shoes are created from Melflex™, a material developed by Melissa, which is malleable and moulds easily to the foot (see page 47). Super-comfortable, these heels can be worn anywhere and for any occasion. They work equally well as a boudoir shoe as when they are teamed with a pretty summer dress. They have a unique sweet smell, as each pair is infused with bubblegum scent.

The Westwood and Melissa brands have collaborated on many shoe designs over the years, with the Lady Dragon Heart being among the most popular. Available in a range of colours, these peep-toe slingbacks display a metallic heart in a contrasting colour as a decoration on the toe. Other adornments found on Westwood Melissa Shoes include bows, cherries and even a globe, which resembles a Christmas bauble. More recently, Velvet Melflex™ has been introduced by Melissa, which has a soft, matte surface similar to flocking, thus giving a richer, more expensive feel to these plastic-based heels.

A far cry from the plastic jelly shoes of the 1980s, these Melissa creations for Vivienne Westwood boast all the right ingredients for accessorizing an edgy on-trend look. Made from a unique material, they are quirky and aesthetic, with unusual embellishments and a top designer name attached, ensuring that this truly unique design captures the imagination.

Kooky

Adornment really can take your heels to a kooky and random level, as the use of outlandish and unexpected materials adds intrigue to a pair of shoes. Simplistic styles decorated in every possible material, object or scene satisfy those with a taste for the bizarre. Only the exhibitionists among us can carry these heels off with panache, but then, these heels should be worn only by those with a gregarious fashion personality.

Dan Sullivan's exclusive Banana Sandwich heels for Irregular Choice epitomize how the use of embellishment can transform a shoe into an extraordinary artistic design. Reminiscent of a night at the opera, the Banana Sandwich shoe is covered with velvet tassels, which move as the wearer walks. Set upon a Harajuku heel, these quirky creations demonstrate how a shoe design can literally take any form or be encrusted with any embellishment in order to pay homage to a specific look.

Sullivan's designs are very tasteful and pretty tame, compared with other kooky compositions that are available for those who love eccentricity. American shoe manufacturer Insa Heels has even used elephant dung to create a sky-high platform sole – an outrageous example of embellishment, resulting in something that the majority of shoe-loving ladies would probably not be happy to wear. Alexander McQueen is another fashion house that experiments with both the shoe silhouette and the embellishment, with some of the more curious designs having been worn by celebrity royalty such as Lady Gaga.

When buying kooky designs, look for those that will add value to your overall appearance, heels that will make a statement in a positive light and get people talking for the right reason. Experiment with your shoes, but remember that these unusual embellishments are not for everyone, so should be worn only by those who want to showcase an extension to their already outgoing personality.

The word 'tassel' derives from the Latin tassau, which refers to the clasp of a necklace.

Artful

Many shoes wouldn't look out of place displayed in a gallery, as they blur the boundaries between fashion and art. Demonstrating intricate workmanship and innovative infusions of colour, style and design, these visually intriguing confections showcase great feats of craftsmanship. Many are wearable designs that only the fashion-forward are confident enough to carry off, but all are admired by those who appreciate heels as miniature works of art for the feet.

Customized

The wedding shoe provides the ultimate opportunity to commission a bespoke design that not only suits the bride's personal style, but that can also become a charming and unique keepsake by which to remember the most special of days. It has become *de rigueur* for those with an artistic eye to customize shoes to reflect the wearer's individuality, which is exactly where Milly J's Shoes excel. I have already introduced you to the stunning one-off shoe creations by this designer, who has a flair for blending creativity with personality (see page 32). Something Blue was designed for one of her clients who loved the idea and style of Milly J's Antique Wedding heels, which displayed pearl beads, a mini tiara, vintage florals and wedding flowers delicately placed on the shoe with shimmering wedding dust and a hand-sewn veil.

For this new design, the wearer, a true romantic at heart with a love of pearls, wanted something unique that captured the essence of her wedding day. Something Blue displayed intricately placed pearls on a baby-blue ground, with the sole and heel decorated with florals. The uniqueness was created in the toe area, in the form of handmade cushions with a gold ring placed on each to signify a ring bearer. Lace, blue and white feathers, and ribbons at the back of the heel completed the transformation from the original beige-patent heel, which Milly J's customized by painting, upholstering and adding delicate beads, bows and, of course, the ring cushions.

Innovative

One of Thea Cadabra's most recognizable designs is the All Weather Shoe, created by the designer in 1978. It is on permanent display in Northampton Museum and Art Gallery, which houses one of the largest shoe collections in the world. These spectacular handmade high-heeled shoes were developed from Cadabra's earlier grey and silver Storm shoes. Broadening the theme, she encompassed the sun, clouds, lightning, rain, a rainbow and blue sky. The rainbow clouds are produced by appliquéd 'Shimmertex', a prismatic plastic reflecting a colour spectrum like the rainbow itself, which wraps around the back of the ankle. A wondrous design of a raging weather scene, these shoes epitomize talented craftsmanship at its best. With this visual feast of sumptuous colours on an avant-garde design, Cadabra has perfectly mastered the essence of how heels can cross over to sculptural artistry.

Novelty

Another of Thea Cadabra's ingenious designs is the Ice Cream sandal, which dates to 1977. This sumptuous, edible-looking shoe was an idea born when the designer was sitting on the top deck of a bus looking down on an ice-cream van, musing on how the shapes of an ice cream and cone could lend themselves to a shoe form, using the cone as the heel and the ice cream as a decorative vamp. The Neapolitan ice-cream scoops are carved from cork and covered with leather and the vertical wafer is wired leather. The chocolate sauce topping is also leather with an embroidered edge, secured with a metal button covered with red patent leather to represent a cherry. The cone heel and main vamp of the peep-toe sandal is covered in handwoven leather, reflecting the look and textured feel of an actual ice-cream cornet. This is a shoe design that is so delicious it really is almost good enough to eat.

Quirky

Funky footwear doesn't get more exciting and quirky than those shoes designed by Dan Sullivan, creator of the Irregular Choice brand. Recently he has stepped away from his mainline range to launch a directional and jaw-dropping collection after his own name. The resulting Dan Sullivan shoes are limited edition and truly one of a kind. Some of the shoes are made by hand with quantities as low as 16 and only one pair in certain sizes. Kooky and diverse designs, they are totally wearable works of art with styles ranging from sky-high platforms to decadent leg spats.

Agasaya 'The Shrieker' was a Semitic war goddess.

The Agasa Trebelina has a carved heel of white-blue Lucite, which sits beneath a lime-green, yellow and hot-pink leg spat. An owl motif adorns the front of the peep-toe shoe and beads strung with feathers decorate the back, which, Sullivan explains, 'ensure you are a true city warrior'.

Another pleasingly bonkers offering from Sullivan is the exotic Got The Hump, a towering gold-coloured wedge heel featuring ChaCha the camel on the side, complete with a gold rope and hot-pink tassel. The main body of the peep-toe shoe displays a colourful Aztec pattern. Last call for the camel ride!

Luxury

Couture shoes exude luxury, individuality and style, especially those made by Caroline Groves, a traditional bespoke shoemaker in the truest sense. In a league of their own, each of her whimsical and romantic shoes are handcrafted at every stage – from the last, which is carved from her client's foot measurements, to the final stitch of embroidered decoration – and finished with an exquisite and unsurpassed attention to detail.

Caroline's interest in shoes was born out of her love for leather, a material of which she has an extensive knowledge. The bespoke white leather boots are made of alum-tawed leather and have a natural vegetable-tanned lining and whitework embroidery. The sole, insole and stiffening are made from English oak-bark-tanned leather. The soles are hand-welted and hand-stitched with natural linen, and the buttons are vintage. The handcrafted heels are carved from beech wood, covered with alum leather and finished with vandyke stitching. Some heels on Caroline's shoes are handcrafted using the historical method of leather stacking, a skilled and expensive process that is rarely used by contemporary shoemakers.

All of Caroline's heavenly creations are a sheer indulgence for those who appreciate shoes as masterpieces. Made to the highest quality with traditional techniques, her heels are spectacular feats of craftsmanship that are impossible to resist.

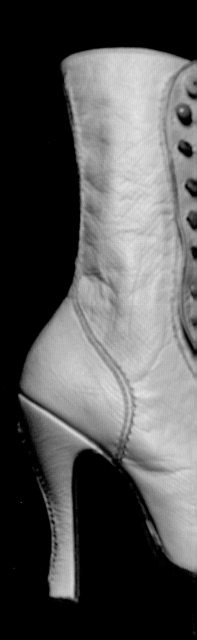

Once seen, never forgotten, Lloraine Neithardt's shoe creations infuse the mystical world and storytelling with elegance and sophistication. A true artisan, her elaborate historical-revival shoes conjure up visions of fairy tales, mystic folk and castles, as well as recapturing times past, when women both embraced and displayed elegance.

Neithardt's shoes are so inspiring that they were featured in the hit 2007 movie *P.S. I Love You*, including the stunning Eros design shown here. This came about because the Oscar-nominated writer and director Richard LaGravenese was inspired to write the film script after admiring Neithardt's designs at her solo art exhibition, The Erotic Life of the Foot: From Soul to Soulier. All the shoes made by Holly, the character played by Hilary Swank in the film, are the work of Neithardt, who designs and makes every pair by hand. She even has a cameo role in the movie as Holly's shoemaking teacher.

'Everyone has a shoe within them.'

Lloraine Neithardt

'Shoes evoke people,' Neithardt elaborates. 'They touch on your consciousness, as they are beautiful both inside and out, thus touching your heart.' A cultural phenomenon, her creations are truly works of art that impress on our mind, body and soul, by taking us on an enchanting journey where anything is possible if we wear shoes that awaken our spirit.

Mystical

Resources

Northampton Museum & Art Gallery
www.northampton.gov.uk/
museums
Tel: 01604 838111
The UK's largest display of
footwear, from ancient times
through to the present day.

V&A Museum
www.vam.ac.uk
London's landmark museum
has shoes forming part of
both their permanent and
temporary exhibitions.

Bourne Collection
www.bournecollection.com
British shoe and accessories
brand committed to producing
affordable luxury and glamour.

Caroline Groves
www.carolinegroves.co.uk
Unique and bespoke
handmade shoes and
handbags for women.

Christian Dior
www.dior.com
Iconic French fashion house.

H&M
www.hm.com
High-street fashion and quality
at an affordable price.

Irregular Choice
www.irregularchoice.com
Owner and designer Dan
Sullivan creates stunning shoes
that stand out from the crowd.

Kat Maconie
www.katmaconie.com
Design-led shoes that fuse
fashion with function.

Kobi Levi
www.kobilevidesign.com
Unique, creative and innovative
'footwear art' from Israel.

Kurt Geiger
www.kurtgeiger.com
Leading the way in footwear
design since 1963, today the
Kurt Geiger studio offers fantasy
footwear and everyday must-
haves through its stores and
concessions worldwide.

Llorraine Neithardt
www.shoefineart.com
Mystical one-of-a-kind shoes
made from rare and precious
materials by this Bronx-born
'shoe artist'.

Milly J's Shoes
www.millyjshoes.co.uk
Multi award-winning avant
garde 'art-to-wear' shoes
loved by celebrities.

Olivia Rubin
www.oliviarubinlondon.com
London-based designer whose
colourful graphic prints feature
on her shoe collections for
Dune (www.dune.co.uk)

PreLoved by *Melina*
Vintage fashion.
36 Amhurst Road
London E8 1JN
Tel: 07591 541564

River Island
www.riverisland.com
Leading fashion retailer.

Selfridges & Co
www.selfridges.com
Historic department store and
home to the Shoe Galleries.
With 55,000 shoes in stock,
it is a shoe lover's heaven.

Thea Cadabra
www.theacadabra.com
Thea's exotic 70s shoes are
now museum exhibits and after
collaborations with Charles
Jourdan and Beverly Feldman
she launched her own label.

Vivienne Westwood
www.viviennewestwood.co.uk
Ingenious and often outrageous
British fashion designer whose
iconic shoes salute fetishism.

Picture Credits

All photography by Terry Benson with the following exceptions:

Eireann / Alamy
Page 15

Chris Everard
Pages 8, 102, 108

Figaro Photo / Gregoire Mahler /
CAMERA PRESS
Page 88

Madame Figaro / Serge Barbeau /
CAMERA PRESS
Page 62

Getty Images
Page 21

Sandra Lane
**Pages 10, 18, 19, 26, 36, 39, 54 insert,
70 insert, 71, 74, 89, endpapers**

Dan Lowe
Pages 120–121

George Marks/ Getty Images
Page 14

Llorraine Neithardt
Pages 122 and 123 insert

Claire Richardson
Backgrounds on pages 45, 70, 92

The Shoe Collection, Northampton Museum & Art
Gallery, Northampton Borough Council
Pages 9, 12, 13, 17, 47

Debi Treloar
Page 77

Kate Whitaker
**Backgrounds on pages 28, 32, 34–35, 43, 50,
53, 54, 58, 64, 69, 73, 84, 87, 95, 98, 105, 107,
115, 119, 123**

Polly Wreford
Pages 4, 7, 31, 69 insert

Index

Acknowledgements

There are so many people I need to thank, as all have contributed in one way or another to this book. My special thanks go to the following:

To my partner Paul who was constantly having to listen to conversations about ladies' high heels, to my mum who took care of my baby boy Harry whilst I wrote about shoes, and my friend Natasha who lent me some of her own gorgeous pairs. To Thea Cadabra, Milly J's, Spoiled Brat, L J Couture, H&M and the Bourne Collection for lending me their wondrous heels to be photographed.

Huge thanks to Luis who styled the shots perfectly and Terry for shooting such amazing photographs, and to his assistant, Jodie, for lending me her wedding shoes before she had even worn them!

Thanks also go to my editor Ellen for all her help and support throughout (although I secretly suspect she too was indulging her own passion for heels!). And to Julia, Cindy and all the team at Ryland Peters & Small for commissioning me to write this book, as I absolutely adore shoes and cannot think of a more pleasurable way of spending my time than being surrounded by towering stilettos in fabulous designs.